JESUS IS MY HELP

DONOVAN O. BROWN

IUNIVERSE, INC.
NEW YORK   BLOOMINGTON

Jesus is My Help

The views expressed in this work are solely those of the author and do not necessarily reflect the views of the publisher, and the publisher hereby disclaims any responsibility for them.

iUniverse books may be ordered through booksellers or by contacting:

iUniverse
1663 Liberty Drive
Bloomington, IN 47403
www.iuniverse.com
1-800-Authors (1-800-288-4677)

Because of the dynamic nature of the Internet, any Web addresses or links contained in this book may have changed since publication and may no longer be valid.

ISBN: 978-1-4401-2911-7 (pbk)
ISBN: 978-1-4401-2912-4 (ebk)

Printed in the United States of America

iUniverse rev. date: 3/3/2009

Lord Jesus you are
neither my bell-
boy, butler or slave.

You are the Lord
God Almighty and
the King over all
kings.

Angels bow before
you, demons flee
from you presence,

death looses its
power at your
command.

You are my God,
my King, my Lord,
my saviour,

my provider, my
deliverer and my
friend.

Hallelujah Jesus,
you are the
Conquering Christ.

Amen

I refuse to die, I
refuse worry and
I refuse to fret for
ever

weapon the enemy
uses against me will
bring me

prosperity and ever
time the powers of
evil attacks me I

will grow stronger.

For every
heartache, every
disaster, every
prison,

every pit I am
convinced that
Jesus will see me

through. And
I know that all
things work
together for

good to them that
love the Lord God,
to them who are

called according to
his purpose.

Hallelujah Jesus

my Lord I can see
the end of these

troubles and trials
and I can see and
declare that all is

well in Jesus name.

Hallelujah Jesus
my Lord and God,
amen.

Jesus hallelujah
to you who is the
Lamb of God

and the conquering
Lion.

You are the Lamb
which was slain for
my sins.

You have set
me free and has
brought me great
joy.

I conquer in your
name Lord.

In the name of
Jesus, amen.

Lord Jesus you
are my mountain
mover, you have
broken

every chain and
removed every
shackle which had
held me

down.

You have set me
free from all my
troubles.

You have brought
me out and
through many fires,
floods,

deep dark and
dangerous valleys.

I love you Lord
and I need you
always in my life

never leave me, be
a fence around me
always.

In the name of
Jesus I ask and
pray.

Amen

Lord Jesus thank
you of ridding my
life of loneliness

by bringing this
precious gift who
is my

wife into my life.

Father thank you
for being faithful
to your promise,

that it is not good
for a man to be
alone and that

you will make a
suitable companion
for him.

Father this gift and
blessing has over
whelmed me with

great joy and
peace.

Father words can
not express my
gratitude to you for

blessing me with
my wife, this your
precious gift to me.

Thank you Lord,

Almighty God for
this precious gift.

In the name of
Jesus I pray.

Amen

Lord Jesus my
mind was in
turmoil and my
heart

in despair, and I
knew why it was
Lord.

It was a direct
consequence of my
disobedience to
your word.

But you Lord out
of your infinite
love and mercy had

not abandoned me.

Out of your
infinite love you
have brought peace
to

my mind and life.

You Lord out of
your infinite love
have taken

all my worries and
troubles and have
put all things right,

which has brought
me great joy, peace

and prosperity.

Lord Jesus from
the depths of my
heart and soul I say
thank

you Lord God
Almighty.

I love you Lord
Jesus, I truly
believe that you are
absolutely

amazing and
wonderful.

In the name of
Jesus I pray and
you give thanks.

Amen

Jehovah, Almighty
God and Father it
is in the

name of Jesus that
I come into your
presence.

You are my light in
the darkest times
and it is you who

have cut and
cleared all my
paths.

Lord you are a
faithful friend to
me, even when I
disobey your

word.

Father thank you
for putting my life
back in order again
and

for instructing me
on the way to go.

Thank you for the
doors and hearts
you have

opened for me to
enter into that will

bring me joy,

peace, security and
prosperity.

You are a faithful
friend and a loving
and merciful God
who

overflows with
grace and mercy.

Thank you for
another chance to
do things right.

It is in the name of
Jesus that I pray.

Amen

Lord Jesus thank
you for not leaving
my mind

and life in a
defragmented and
scattered state.

Lord you showed
up when I called
out to you,
beseeching your

help and you
brought the answer
of heaven to solve
the

problems which
I faced here on
earth.

Lord Jesus when
you had finished
there was a

miracle in my life.

Lord Jesus thank
you for opening up
the grave I was in
and

giving me life and
setting me free.

Lord you have

rebuked the enemy
for my sake, you
brought

me back from the
dead, you Lord
have set my family

free from
unhappiness.

Thank you Lord
Jesus for showing
up in my situation
and

destroying the
agent and agenda
of the devil and
giving me

my family back to
me.

Hallelujah Jesus,
glory to God in the
highest.

Thank you Lord
for another chance.

Thank you for
putting my life in
order again.

In Jesus name I
pray and thank you

Lord.

Amen

Thank you Lord
Jesus for hearing
my plea for help
and coming

to my rescue.

Lord had you not
come to my aid I
would have been
lost,

my troubles would
have consumed my
life.

But Lord in your
presence there are
no impossibilities,
what is

impossible for man
is possible for you
to accomplish.

My God you came
into my life and
accomplished the

impossible.

Hallelujah Jesus,
hallelujah Lord.

Thank you Lord
Jesus for you love
for me and you

grace and

patience when I go
astray.

Thank you
for doing the
impossible for me
which has brought

me great joy and
peace.

Thank you my
Lord and God.

In the name of
Jesus I pray.

Amen

Jehovah, Almighty
God and Father
you have brought
me into

your kingdom and
have lavished your
love upon me and

surround me with
your presence. You
have shown me

wonderful and
amazing things.

You have given
me the power to
trample the power
of the

enemy and nothing
can harm me.

You have greatly
honoured me even
though it is you
who

deserve to be
honoured and
praised.

Father you love for
me has no bounds,
I welcome you
Lord in

my heart and my
life.

Come in and lead
me, take control of
my troubles.

Thank you my
Father,

it is in the name of
Jesus that I ask and
pray.

Amen

Lord Jesus thank
you for putting my
life together again
when it

was defragmented
and scattered.

It was due to the
disobedience of
your word that I
allowed the

devil to come into
my life to kill, steal
and destroy.

Lord forgive me of
my misdeeds in the
name of Jesus I ask.

Jesus when I was
in the gutters you
were with me and
had not

abandoning me to
sin.

Thank you Lord
for renewing my
mind with you
word and

changing my life
and leading me out
of those terrible

circumstances
victoriously.

Thank you Lord
for giving back to
me what the devil
stole,

thank you Lord for
resurrecting what
the devil killed in
my life

and thank you
Lord for restoring
what he had
destroyed.

Jesus truly you
are amazing and
wonderful, thank
you Lord.

It is in the name of
Jesus that I pray.

Amen

Lord Jesus,
merciful and loving
God,

I turn to you and
no one else for
help, for with you
nothing is

impossible.

I can shout and
declare my troubles
over when I bring
them to

you in prayer.

I can have peace of
mind when I bring
all my troubles

to you in prayer.

When I bring my
troubles in prayer
to you I can leave
with

great joy knowing
they are gone.

For you have
the power and
authority to put all
things right

and you will put all

things right for you
are a loving and
faithful

God who do not
want me to suffer.

Lord Jesus I leave
all my troubles in
your hands and I
declare

them over.

Thank you for
victory my Lord.

It is in the name of
Jesus that I pray.

Amen

Lord Jesus one of
the most important
thing you have
done for

me was to set my
mind free with
your word.

You have renewed
my mind and in
doing so you have
set me

free, which has
caused me to live
in abundance.

You have set me
free from the limits
fear had bounded
me to.

Thank you Lord
Jesus for renewing
my mind with you
word

and setting me free
from the shackles
which the enemy
had

over my mind
which had caused
me to live in
bondage and

poverty.

Truly I have that
what you came
from glory to give
to me

which is life and
life in abundance.

Thank you Lord
for renewing my
mind.

It is in the name of
Jesus that I pray.

Amen

Lord Jesus why
should I worry?

Why should I fret?

You Lord are the
all-powerful and
all-knowing God,
you are

also loving and
faithful; and on
your promises I can
depend.

You have promised
me hope and
a bright and
prosperous

future.

Though weeping
may last for the
night I know you
will bring

me joy in the
morning.

Thank you Lord
Jesus for my joy
and victories.

Hallelujah Jesus,
for my joy and
victories.

It is in the name
of Jesus that I pray
and give thanks.

Amen.

Lord Jesus you
have declared to
me,

"You are my
servant; I have
chosen you and
have not

rejected you.

Do not be afraid;
for I am with
you: do not be
frightened;

for I am your God:
I will strengthen
you; I will help
you;

I will uphold you
with righteousness.

Observe, all those
who were furious
with you will be

ashamed and
puzzled: they will
be as nothing; and
them

that fight against
you will perish.

You will seek them,

and will not find
them, even those

that challenge and
war against you
will be as nothing."

Lord Jesus thank
you for your
promise and
protection.

In the name of
Jesus I pray.

Amen

Lord Jesus you had
allowed trouble to
come into my life

which had
disrupted my peace
of mind.

Lord it is good that
you allowed this to
happen for it had

forced me to seek
your presence.

It has caused me
to pray more
and rekindle our
relationship

which had gone
cold.

Lord you saved my
life and secured
my prosperity yet
again.

Lord Jesus truly
you are a loving
God and a faithful
friend,

please forgive me
of the sins I have
committed and
thank you

for everything
including the
storms.

It is in the name
of Jesus that I pray
and thank you
Lord.

Amen.

Lord Jesus, thank
you for never
leaving me and for
always

protecting and
guiding me. You
are truly wonderful
and

amazing.

You are more than
just the King of
kings, you are more
than

just Lord over all,
you are more than
my way-maker and

mountain mover,
you are more than
just my refuge, you
are

more than just
my provider you
are the Everlasting
Father,

the Prince of Peace
and Mighty God.

Hallelujah Jesus,
hallelujah my Lord,
hallelujah Jesus my

mountain mover,
hallelujah Jesus my
provider, deliverer
and

God.

Lord you are
excellent and
wonderful and
worthy of all glory

honour and praise.

Hallelujah Jesus,
hallelujah Most
High God.

In Jesus name.

Amen

Jesus, All-powerful
and loving God.

Thank you for
fighting my battles
and giving me the
victories.

Lord Jesus what is
impossible for man
is possible for you,

for in your
presence there are
no impossibilities,

you Lord can never
fail.

You are the Alpha
and Omega the
beginning and the
end

You Lord will
be with me at
the beginning of
trouble and see

me through to the
end.

You are truly
awesome and
amazing and I am
glad that

you chose me and
is present in my
life.

In Jesus name,
amen.

Lord Jesus the
attack which you
have allowed to be
launched

upon my life is
difficult indeed and
it is taking a toll on
me.

Lord I know that
all things will work
out for my benefit
in the

end, but I ask you
for the strength
and peace of mind
to

weather this storm.

I know that you are
with me and will
not allow things I
can not

bear to come upon
me.

Please Lord
strengthen and
help me through
this difficult time.

In the name of
Jesus I ask.

Amen

Lord Jesus, I come to you in this my hour of need for help.

Lord please come to my rescue and deliver me out of all these

troubles.

Lord Jesus please come now to my aid, come in your glory and

your power and resolve all my troubles.

Lord I turn to you for it is only you who can save me.

Lord it is only you who can heal the wounded, mend the

broken, restore the shattered and save the lost.

Lord Jesus come now to my rescue I need you Lord.

It is in the name of
Jesus ask and pray.

Amen

I plead the blood
of Jesus over
my mind, my
emotions,

my family, my
home, my finances,
my property and
my

workplace, in the
name of Jesus.

In the name of
Jesus I rebuke
you Satan and all
principalities

and powers of
darkness which
have invaded my
life, my home,

my family, my
workplace.

And I command
you in the name of
Jesus to cease your

activities and be
now removed.

In the name of
Jesus.

Jehovah, eternal
Father and most
high God,

thank you for the
privilege of being
able to come into
your

presence through
your son Jesus.

Father you are
merciful and
awesome, loving
and kind, faithful

and just and full of
grace.

In your presence
there are only tears
of joy and cries of

overwhelming
happiness.

Hallelujah Jehovah,
wonderful and
excellent God,
merciful and

loving Father.

Hallelujah Jehovah
wonderful and
excellent God, you

deserve

to be lifted up,
glorified and
honour you are
truly worthy of

praise.

Hallelujah Jehovah,
most high God,
faithful and loving

friend.

You are truly
wonderful and
excellent, Lord.

In Jesus name,
amen.

Jehovah my God,
it is in the name of
Jesus that I come
into

your presence.

Merciful and
loving God,
hallelujah,
hallelujah most
high God.

Father thank
you for levelling
mountains and
removing

obstacles which
stood before me
which hindered my
progress,

prosperity and
happiness.

Father you have
used what the
enemy meant to
harm and

hinder me to bless
and prosper me.

Almighty God
thank you for
sending your word

to heal, rescue

deliver and help
me.

Father you word
has made rough
places smooth for
me to

travel and has lead
me to wonderful
places and has
brought

me into connection
with wonderful
people.

Hallelujah Jehovah
my Father and
God you are truly
wonderful

and amazing.

Hallelujah Jehovah
my Lord and
God you are truly
wonderful

and amazing.

In Jesus name,
amen.

Lord Jesus thank
you for giving me
joy and peace of
mind even

in the midnight
hour. You have
strengthened me
and have

brought my life
back on the right
track

Lord Jesus thank
you for your grace
and favour for if I
have

your favour even
my enemies have
to favour me.

Lord thank you
for loving me even
when I was lost in
sin.

Thank you for
wooing me to you,
bringing me into
your

kingdom of life,
great joy and peace.

Lord Jesus, King of

kings, I thank you
from the depths of
my

heart. You are
wonderful and
excellent and I
thank you for

being a part of my
life.

Hallelujah Jesus,
hallelujah my Lord.

It is in the name
of Jesus that I
pray and give you
thanks.

Amen

I declare in the
name of Jesus that
from this day forth
I am the

head and not the
tail, I am above
only and not
beneath.

Wherever I go I
will prosper and
whatever I do will
prosper

and every weapon
forged to harm me
will never prosper.

I am blessed in
the city, blessed in
the country, I am
blessed

when I get up and
when I lay down.

I am blessed when
I come in and
when I go out.

I am blessed and
highly favoured by
Jesus who is the
Lord of

hosts.

All these I declare
in the name of
Jesus.

Amen

Lord Jesus
promotion comes
neither from the
north or south

neither from east
or west but from
you.

It is you who have
promoted and
prospered me in
life and it is

you who has given
me favour with
others wherever I
go.

Great is you love
and faithfulness
Lord Jesus, great is
you love

and faithfulness to
me.

Your have never
let me down, great
and true is your
love and

faithfulness to me.

Lord Jesus you
have brought me to
levels greater and

richer

which has far
exceeded my
imagination.

You have promoted
to this level filled
with privileges fit
for a

great kings.

Thank you Lord
Jesus for promoting
me and causing
me to

prosper on this
earth.

Thank you Lord, in
Jesus name.

Amen

Lord Jesus you
said, "If you
remain in me, and
my words

live in you, you
will ask what you
will, and it will be
done

for you."

Lord, you know
that I believe and
trust in your word
and

your Holy Spirit
lives in me.

So Lord according
to you word I ask
in the name of
Jesus

that you bind and
break every power
of evil in my life

and in the life of
my family.

Rebuke the spirits
of evil for my sake,
Lord Jesus and

cause me to

succeed and
prosper not only
prosper

spiritually but
materially and
financially.

Release the
promised covenant
blessings promised
to the

descendants of
Abraham in my
life, right now Lord
Jesus.

Please Lord, cause
poverty to leave my
life and restore

my good health
now, Lord Jesus.

It is in the name of
Jesus that I ask and
say thanks.

Amen

Lord Jesus it is to
you that I give the
glory and praise,

for the devil came
in and took my joy
and peace.

I was in deep
despair and I cried
out to you for help
and you

showed up
and took all my
problems and
defeated my

enemies and
restored my joy
and my peace and
gave me

hope.

Jesus, merciful God
and Lord, I lift you
up and I praise and

worship you for all
you have done just
for me.

Blessed is your
name, blessed be
the name of Jesus.

Lord you are the
conquering Christ.

Hallelujah Jesus
my Lord and God,
thank you.

In Jesus name,
amen.

Lord Jesus you saw
me when I was
down and lifted me
up.

When I was in the
deep dark valley
you took me and
placed

me on top of the
highest mountain.

When I was dead
in sin you bled and
died to set me free
and

give me everlasting
life and life in all
its abundance.

Lord you have
cleaned up all the
mess which had
settled in my

life and has blessed
me greatly.

Lord your
love for me is
overwhelming, my
life is richly blessed

for you are with
me.

Thank you Lord
for everything.

In Jesus name,
amen.

Lord Jesus
please give me
insight, wisdom,
knowledge and

understanding so
that I will live my
life effectively and

fruitfully on this
earth.

Bless my
endeavours Lord
and cause them to
prosper.

Be my light and
my guide for I can
not succeed on my
own,

I need your
direction, your
favour and your
council.

Thank you for your
Holy Spirit which
lives in me,

Jesus you are
a loving and
wonderful God.

Thank you Lord
for everything and

for answering my
prayers.

In the name of
Jesus I pray.

Amen.

Lord Jesus you
are my friend and
brother, please
forgive me of

the sins that I have
committed as I
come into your
presence.

Lord you are
wonderful and
excellent, faithful
and just.

You are the Mighty
God.

Lord Jesus thank
you for fighting
my battles on my
behalf and

though it may
appear at this
moment as if I am
defeated I

believe in my heart
that victory is
mine. I know in
my heart

and confess with
my mouth victory
is mine no matter
how

things appear.

For you are a God
who can never
fail and in your
presence

there are no
impossibilities.

You Lord bring life
where was death,
victory where there
was

defeat, joy where
there was sorrow
and hope where
was

despair.

Lord Jesus
hallelujah,
hallelujah my God.

Because of you
Lord I declare
myself victorious,
thank you

Lord for giving me
victory.

In Jesus name,
amen.

Lord Jesus you
are a trustworthy
witness, the
firstborn of

the dead and the
Prince of the kings
of the earth.

To you Lord who
always love us and
has loosed and
freed

us from our sins by
your own blood,
and has made us

kings and priests
unto God the
Father; to you be
glory

and dominion for
ever and ever.

In Jesus name,
amen.

Jehovah, my
heavenly Father
and God I come to
you in

the name of Jesus.

Father because of
your great love for
me, you, who is
rich

in mercy, has made
me alive with
Christ Jesus even
when

I was dead in
transgressions—it
is by your grace
that I

have been saved.

You raised me up
with Christ Jesus
and has seated me

with you in the
heavenly realms in
Christ Jesus.

You have given me
power to trample
upon serpents and

scorpions and over
all the power of the
enemy, and

nothing can harm
me.

Hallelujah Jehovah,
my loving God and
Father.

Hallelujah Jehovah,
my Father, you are
marvellous.

In Jesus name,
amen.

Ministering angels
of Jehovah the true
and Almighty God

I command you in
the in the name of
Jesus bring now

into my life from
the east, from the
west, from the
north

and from the south
all the blessings,
treasures and

wealth which
Almighty God has

placed on this earth
for me and bring
back to me

everything which
the forces of evil
has stolen from
me.

Do this now
ministering angels
I command you in
the

name of Jesus.

Lord Jesus thank
you for being a
very present source
of

help during my
times of trouble
and for rising up a

standard against
the enemy when he
comes in like a

flood against me.

Lord thank you for
your mercy and
grace, for freedom

and victory.

Hallelujah Jesus,
hallelujah Jesus

In Jesus name,
amen

Lord Jesus your
blood has washed
away all my sins
and

testifies before
the thrown of
Almighty God that
I am

redeemed from sin
and death and has
been made a child

of the Most High
God.

Lord cover me and
my family with you
blood, let it cover

our enemies
and burn up and
destroy the hold
and the

works of all
demonic forces in
our lives and wash
them

away.

Hallelujah Jesus,
hallelujah Lord,
than you for your

precious blood.

In the name of I
pray Jesus name,
amen.

I declare victory
mine,

I declare joy mine,

I declare peace
mine,

I declare
financial
dominion and
prosperity
mine in

the mighty
name of Jesus.

I declare
that every
weapon and
manoeuvres
of the

powers of
darkness
which has
come to
destroy and

hinder me and
my family will
fail in their
purpose.

I am above only
not beneath and
wherever I go I will

prosper in the
mighty name of
Jesus.

Amen

I come against
every demonic
spirit which has
come

against me and my
family in the name
of Jesus and I cast

you out in the
name of Jesus.

Lord Jesus thank
you for the name
of Jesus, for the
name

of Jesus which
has all-power and
authority.

Thank you Lord
for the privilege of
being able to use

your name.

Your name brings
peace, victory,
hope, life, freedom,

prosperity and
great happiness.

I declare peace,
victory, life,
happiness,

freedom and
prosperity mine in
the name of Jesus.

Amen

When the spirits of
evil comes in like a
flood against me

and my family the
Holy Spirit will
raise up a standard

against them.

So I come against
the powers of
darkness and their

attacks on my life
in the name of
Jesus and I repel
ever

attack on my life
and on my family
in the name

of Jesus.

I rebuke you Satan
and every power of
evil which has

come against me
and my family in
the name of Jesus.

I break you hold
over our minds,
and bind your
works

and cast you and
your demonic
spirits out of our
lives

now in the name of
Jesus.

Hallelujah Jesus
thank you for
trampling and
defeating

the forces of
darkness which has
come against me
and

my family.

Hallelujah Jesus,
thank you Lord my
God.

In Jesus name,
amen.

Holy Spirit of the
true and living
God rise up and
shine

forth now in my
life, in Jesus name
I ask.

Rebuke and cast
out the devil and
every spirit of evil
in

my life and family
in the mighty
name of Jesus.

Holy Spirit you are
not a spirit of fear
instead you are a

holy spirit a spirit
of power and love
an all conquering

spirit one that can
never fail.

Holy Spirit rise up
and shine now and
defeat the powers

of darkness
operating in my
life and my family.

Rise up and shine
now in me Holy
Spirit in the
mighty

name of Jesus I ask.

Hallelujah Jesus.

Amen

Jehovah my God
and Father,

hallelujah Most
High God

Jehovah Most High
God hallelujah.

Thank you for
washing and
renewing my mind
with your

word. Father your
word has set me
free not only from
sin

and death but also
from shyness and
low self-esteem.

I have become
bolder than a lion,
your word has set
my

mind free from the
sense of inferiority
which the devil

had deposited and
cultivated in my
mind, which had
held

me back from
achieving my full
potential.

I now see myself as
you word says, as
the head and not

the tail as above
only and not
beneath, rich and
not poor

and more than
a conquer in all
things.

I am not arrogant
but now bold,
confident and

successful, thank
you Father for your
word and its

continuous work
in me.

In Jesus name I
pray, amen.

Plead my case Lord
Jesus,

Fight against all
who fight against
me.

Come to my help
and rescue from all
these troubles.

Lord I believe that
you will deliver me
safely.

Lord Jesus bless my
life with all good
things and thank

you for you grace,
your mercy and
help.

Thank you Lord
for everything in
Jesus name I pray.

Amen.

Hallelujah Jesus,
hallelujah Lord,

wonderful
councillor and
mighty God.

It is to you I give
the glory and praise
for the victories in

my life. I called
and you answered,
I requested in
prayer

and you acted on
my behalf.

Lord I am so glad
for what you have
done for me, I was
in

disperse and my
mind in total
confusion.

I brought all my
troubles to you
in prayer and you
helped

me and healed me
and put all things
right.

Hallelujah Jesus,
hallelujah my Lord,

you have achieved
the impossible for
me; you have done

what I and no one
else could have
done.

Thank you Lord
for working things
out in my favour.

In Jesus name,
amen

Jehovah, All-
mighty God and
Father I come to
you in the

name of Jesus.
Father release your
Holy Spirit upon
this

city, let your Spirit
invade lives all over
this city and

rescue souls.

Where there is
turmoil bring
peace, where there
is hurt

and sorrow bring
healing and great
joy, where there is

death let your
Spirit bring new
life.

Lord let your
spirit invade our
communities and
homes

and fight against
forces of darkness
which have

invaded

our families.

Rescue us from the
powers of darkness
and lead us.

Hallelujah Jehovah
my God you are
wonderful my
God.

Hallelujah Father,
in Jesus name I
pray.

Amen.

Jehovah my God,

who is rich in
mercy, it is because
of Your great love
for

me, you have made
me alive with
Christ Jesus even

when I was dead in
transgressions—it
is by your grace

that I have been
saved.

You have raised
me up with Christ
Jesus and has
seated

me with him in the
heavenly realms.

Praise be to you
Jehovah the God
and Father of my
Lord

Jesus Christ, who
has blessed me in
the heavenly realms

with every spiritual
blessing in Christ
Jesus. For you
chose

me in him before
the creation of the
world to be holy
and

blameless in Your
sight.

Glory be to you
and blessed be your
name

Jehovah my God.

In Jesus name,
amen.

Jehovah my Father,
I come to you in
the name of Jesus.

Hallowed be
your name Father
hallowed be your
name.

Father let your will
be done in my life
as your will is done

in heaven.

Father your will is
for me to prosper
in all things even as

my soul prospers.
Father your will is
that I must have
life

and live in
abundance of all
good things. Father
it is your

will for me to have
love, joy, peace,
children and
wealth.

Father it is your
will to make me
the head and not

the tail

to place me on top
and not beneath.
Father it is your
will

that I prosper
wherever I go
and to prosper in
whatever I

do. Father it is
your will that I
have dominion
over the

powers of evil.
Father it is your
will to go before
me and

remove all obstacles
and open doors to
give me the

treasures of
darkness and
hidden riches in
secret places.

Father let you will
be done in my life
now in the name of

Jesus, amen.

I receive now in my
life the promised
covenant blessings

to the descendants
of Abraham in the
name of Jesus.

I receive now in
my life financial
blessings and
prosperity

in the name of
Jesus. I receive my
blessings from the

east in the name of
Jesus. I receive my
blessings

from west in the
name of Jesus.
I receive my
blessings

from north in the
name of Jesus. I
receive my

blessings from
south in the name
of Jesus. In the
name

of Jesus I receive
my properties with

interest which the

powers of evil had
stolen from me.

I declare in the
name of Jesus that
I am a child of

Jehovah the true
and living God,
and I receive all my

blessings now in
the name of Jesus.

Amen.

Jehovah my Father,
come in and
change my life
Lord.

Stir up the talents
which you have
deposited

in me and cause
me to be fruitful.

Father, open
doors of great
opportunities for
me so that I can

improve my life
and enlarge my
territory greatly.

Close doors in my
life which needs to
be shut and break
down

barriers which
separate me from
my blessings and
build

barriers which
needs to be in
place.

Lord, help me and
direct me; deliver

me safely from the

powers of evil.

In the name of
Jesus I ask and
pray.

Amen

Jesus you are the
resurrection and
the life and anyone

who believes in you
will not die or be
disappointed.

Lord you are
stronger than I,
you have rescued
my family

from the clutches
and power of evil
and have brought

them back to me
something I or
anyone else could

accomplish.

Thank you Lord
for delivering my
family from evil
and

making us stronger
and bringing us
closer than ever.

Thank you Lord
for the lessons
learnt and the
hurdles we

overcame.

Thank you Jesus,
hallelujah Lord, in
Jesus name I pray.

Amen

Lord Jesus, your
Holy Spirit has
come into my life
and has

transformed my
life.

Your Spirit has
brought me from
death to life,

from defeat to
victory, from
tragedy to triumph,
from

poverty to great
wealth, from
sickness to good
health

and wholeness.

Lord your Spirit
has gathered all the
pieces of my life

which was scattered
and has brought
them back together

and has put all the
pieces in order.

Lord you Spirit has
given me new life

and new strength.

Hallelujah Jesus
thank you Lord, in
the name of Jesus

name, amen.

Satan you and the
principalities and
the powers and the

rulers of the
darkness and
the spiritual
wickedness in

high places and the
demonic spirits the
blood of Jesus is

against you in my
life, the blood of
Jesus is against you
in

my job, the blood
of Jesus is against
you in my family,

the blood of Jesus
is against you in
my business, the

blood of Jesus is
against you over
my property.

Satan and all
powers of evil the
blood of Jesus
speaks to

your destruction
and my

deliverance,
salvation and

victory in the name
of Jesus.

Jehovah my Father
I come to you in
the name of Jesus.

Father you have
given me the power
to create wealth, so

Father in the name
of Jesus stir up the
talents and gifts

which you have
deposited in my
life, and help me to

make the
maximum use of all
the opportunities
which

you have create for
me and lead me to
and through the

doors which you
have opened for
me so that I can
create

great wealth. In the
name of Jesus I ask.

Father bring into
my life the people
and bring me to
the

organizations
which will help
me to achieve my
purpose

and remove all
obstacles which
will try to hinder
me.

Father thank you
for answering my
prayer in the name
of

Jesus, amen.

Jehovah my Father
in heaven I come
to you in the name

of Jesus. Father you
say ask and it will
be

given seek and you
will find and knock
and the door will

be opened for you.
So Father in the
name of Jesus I ask

you to please help
me and give me the
necessary tools,

skills, advice and
resources to start
and run my own

business
successfully and
profitably.

Father thank you
for answering this
prayer and for the

what you are about
to do in my life. I
thank you in

advance for the

birthing and the
success of my
company.

It is to you I
give the glory
and thanks for
achieving this. It

is you who has
given me the desire
and vital resources

and help to birth
this business and
it is your favour
which

has caused it and
me to prosper. It is
you who has given

me to power and
help to create this
wealth.

Father thank you,
it is in Jesus name I
pray, amen.

Jehovah my God I
come to you in the
name of Jesus.

Father I ask you in
the name of Jesus
to anoint me and

help me to succeed
give me ideas to act
upon so that I

will prosper on this
earth.

Give me your
favour so that I
may have favour
with

others and prosper
wherever I go and
bless my

endeavours so that
I will be free from
ceaseless toil.

Father enlarge my
territory release
right now your

supernatural favour
upon my life.
Cause me to have

unnatural success,

cause miracles to
come into my life.

As you open the
windows of heaven
over my life cause

wealth to flow
from the east, west,
north and south
into

my life in the name
of Jesus I ask.

Father in heaven I
have done my best
only you can do

the rest.

In the name of
Jesus I pray, amen.

Jehovah my Father
and God I come to
you in the name of

Jesus. Father please
forgive me of all
the sins that I have

committed.

Father I come to
for help and ask
you in the name of

Jesus to break
down barriers and
open doors which

separates me from
your blessings.

Father lead me and
guide me cause me
to be fruitful,

cause success to
overwhelm my life
in all things.

It is in the name of
Jesus that I ask and
pray, amen.

Lord Jesus I lift up
mine eyes to you
from where my

Help comes. My
help comes you the
Lord, who has

made heaven and
earth.

Lord you will not
suffer my foot to
be moved and you

never slumber nor
sleep.

Lord Jesus you are
my keeper: you are
the shade upon

my right hand.
The sun will never
smite me by day,

nor the moon by
night.

You preserve me
from all evil: you
will

preserve my soul.

Lord Jesus you
preserve my
going out and my
coming in

always and even for
evermore.

In Jesus name,
amen

Lord Jesus I see
you as high and
lifted up full of
power

and glory. Lord
you are greater
than all these
troubles

which has invaded
my life.

Because I have
presented these
troubles to you in
faith I

believe in the end
I will win and will
be lifted up.

Because I called
upon you in the
name of Jesus no

weapon can destroy
me and no enemy
can defeat me

because you are my
help, you are my
deliverer, you are

my provider, you
are my strength.
You are my God

who is

high and lifted up
and my confidence
in you will not be

disappointed.

In Jesus name I
pray and give you
thanks, amen.

Jesus come into
my life and be my
Lord, please forgive

me of all the sins
which I have
committed. Come
in and

through your Holy
Spirit change me.

Lead me according
to your will and
purpose.

Jesus I accept you
as my Lord and
saviour and I know
you

have accepted me
also.

Thank you Lord in
Jesus name I pray,
amen.

For I am
convinced, that
neither death, nor
life, nor

angels, nor
principalities, nor
powers, nor things
present,

nor things to come,
nor height, nor
depth, nor any
other

creature, can to
separate us from
the love of God,
which

is in Christ Jesus
our Lord. But
because of his great
love

for us, God, who
is rich in mercy,
made us alive with

Christ Jesus even
when we were dead
in transgressions—

it is by grace we
have been saved.
And God raised us
up

with Christ Jesus
and seated us
with him in the
heavenly

realms in Christ
Jesus.

Praise be to the
God and Father
of our Lord Jesus
Christ,

who has blessed
us in the heavenly
realms with every

spiritual blessing
in Christ. For he
chose us in him
before

the creation of the
world to be holy
and blameless in
his

sight in love

In Jesus name,
amen

Lord Jesus the
spirits of darkness
and evil came into
my

life and destroyed
my past.

Thank you for
now, Lord, I am
high and lifted up,
for you

came into my life
and gave me hope,
a new beginning,

a bright and
prosperous present
and future.

No one who comes
to you Lord will
die or ever be

disappointed.
Lord Jesus you
resurrected my soul
for

death, you restored
my joy, you
promoted me in
life and

has given me power
over the forces of

evil.

You have
transformed me
from a victim to a
victor and

has brought me
into the kingdom
of the Jehovah our

Father who is the
Holy God.

Hallelujah Jesus
and thank you
Lord, blessed be
your

name.

In Jesus name I
pray, amen